The
Poe

DALESMAN BOOKS

THE DALESMAN PUBLISHING COMPANY LTD.,
CLAPHAM, VIA LANCASTER, LA2 8EB
First published 1980
Second edition 1983
Reprinted 1985, 1988

ISBN: 0 85206 709 7

WILLIAM WORDSWORTH
AS AN OLD MAN

Printed by Fretwell & Cox Ltd., Goulbourne Street, Keighley, West Yorkshire.

LOUGHRIGG TARN AND LANGDALE PIKES

Contents

Illustrations

T. Parker: *Colour Picture,* 1, 3, 8, 17, 21, 22, 25, 30, 36, 38, 39, 43, 44, 47, 51, 56, 67, 87, 89. **National Portrait Gallery:** Cover Portrait of Wordsworth. **Kenneth Scowen:** 4, 62. **F. Leonard Jackson:** 7, 12, 49, 72. **Noel Habgood:** 10. **Ivor Nicholas:** 14. **G. V. Berry:** 26. **Tom Taylor:** 29. **Derek Widdicombe:** 35, 50, 52, 53, 55, 71. **John H. Whalley:** 40. **William F. Meadows:** 54. **Leslie Sansom:** 57, 68. **Frank and Molly Partington:** 64. **Arthur Gilpin:** 70. **W. R. Mitchell:** 79, 83. **A. N. Jefferies:** 92.

An Introduction

TOWARDS THE END of the 18th century, during what we now call the Romantic Period, the Lake District was visited by some perceptive travellers, seekers after "natural curiosities." Many of them left us a record, in prose or verse, of what they saw and experienced. Their impressions were limited, their phrases rather stilted, and they quoted freely from classical authors.

When a young poet, William Wordsworth, returned to his native district in 1799, he was aware of a revolutionary fervour in Europe that was sweeping away the old classicism. For him, a dazzling new world began at the very doorstep of Dove Cottage, Grasmere. His study was not a musty room, but in the great out-doors, where he contemplated the grandeur of Nature and the human condition, writing down his thoughts with a passionate simplicity. He became aware, through mystical experience, of realms which lay beyond the solid world that confronted him on every walk he took.

While "sitting on the stones, feasting in silence" he was moved emotionally by the commonplace:

Thanks to the human heart by which we live;
Thanks to its tenderness, its joys and fears;
To me, the meanest flower that blows can give
Thoughts that do often lie too deep for tears.

Opposite: Road to Wrynose Pass.

He could also write a resounding hymn of praise:

Yet were I grossly destitute of all
Those human sentiments that make this earth
So dear, if I should fail with grateful voice
To speak of you, ye mountains and ye lakes
And sounding cataracts, ye mist and winds
That dwell among the hills where I was born.

Friends and devotees were drawn to the heart of Lakeland by Wordsworth's presence. They saw the Lake District in an exquisitely beautiful phase of development, when the works of Nature and of man were still in balance. Man had not yet got the upper hand. Wordsworth and Samuel Taylor Coleridge, who had a similar revelation of a fresh new world of thought and experience, were joined by Robert Southey and, in due course, as residents or occasional visitors, by De Quincey, Shelley, Lamb and Keats. Another Lakeland resident of note was the ebullient John Wilson, of Elleray, who became renowned as the writer "Christopher North" in *Blackwood's Magazine*. Wordsworth, Coleridge and Southey were the three men in the mind of a writer in the *Edinburgh Review* of 1817; he mentioned, mockingly, the "Lake School," from which was derived an honourable term, The Lake Poets.

Wordsworth needed the stimulation – even the praise – of sympathetic friends. He received it from his sister Dorothy and from Coleridge. Charles Lamb ventured north to Keswick in 1802. Keats was here in 1818. Shelley spent a three-month honeymoon at a cottage overlooking Keswick in 1811-12. De Quincey's brilliant penmanship gave us a first-hand account of the doings of the Poets. Walter Scott visited Lakeland and, of course, he spent some time with the Wordsworths.

Examples of the work of The Lake Poets appear in this book. Also represented are poems by later writers: by John Ruskin, who purchased Brantwood, by Coniston Water, in 1871; Canon H. D. Rawnsley, for long vicar of Crosthwaite, who later settled in Grasmere, and others. Yet it is of the original Poets we mainly think: of that feverishly-brilliant group who, early in the 19th century, poured out their feelings in memorable verse. Wordsworth alone is said to have written 70,000 lines of poetry. The freshness of much of his verse inspires us still . . .

W. R. MITCHELL

The Earth Awakens

A Dale in March

The Cock is crowing,
The stream is flowing,
The small birds twitter,
The lake doth glitter,
The green field sleeps in the sun;
The oldest and youngest
Are at work with the strongest;
The cattle are grazing,
Their heads never raising;
There are forty feeding like one!

Like an army defeated
The snow hath retreated,
And now doth fare ill
On the top of the bare hill;
The ploughboy is whooping – anon – anon
There's joy in the mountains;
There's life in the fountains;
Small clouds are sailing,
Blue sky prevailing;
The rain is over and gone!

WILLIAM WORDSWORTH
Written near Brotherswater

Daffodils

I wandered lonely as a cloud
That floats on high o'er vales and hills,
When all at once I saw a crowd,
A host, of golden daffodils;
Beside the lake, beneath the trees,
Fluttering and dancing in the breeze.

Continuous as the stars that shine
And twinkle on the milky way,
They stretched in never-ending line
Along the margin of a bay:
Ten thousand saw I at a glance,
Tossing their heads in sprightly dance.

The waves beside them danced; but they
Out-did the sparkling waves in glee:
A poet could not but be gay,
In such a jocund company; .
I gazed – and gazed – but little thought
What wealth the show to me had brought:

For oft, when on my couch I lie
In vacant or in pensive mood,
They flash upon that inward eye
Which is the bliss of solitude;
And then my heart with pleasure fills,
And dances with the daffodils.

WILLIAM WORDSWORTH
His best-known poem was inspired
by daffodils seen near Ullswater.

Opposite: Borrans Field, Windermere.

A Song of Spring

Come! sweet April, whom all men praise,
Bring your daffodils up to the Raise,
Bid the delicate warbler trill,
Come with the cuckoo over the hill
Sprinkle the birch with sprays of green,
Purple the copses all between;
Bend the rainbow, and swell the brooks,
Fill the air with the sound of rooks,
Rubies lend, for the larch to wear,
The lambs are bleating, and May is near.

August comes, and the speckled thrush
Sings no more in the lilac bush,
Lambs in the meadow cease to bleat,
The hills are dim with the noontide heat,
From all her hedges the rose is fled,
And only the harebell lifts her head;
But green are the new-mown vales with grass
As if the Spring were again to pass,
And children bring from the far-off fell
The rose-red heather – the bee loves well,

Comes October with breath more cold,
She breathes, and the bracken turns to gold,
The cherry blushes as red as blood,
The rowan flames in the painted wood,
The larch-tree tresses are amber bright,
The birch is yellowing up on the height,
And over the valley and over the hill
A deep hush broods and the sheep are still,
But rainbow gossamers fill the air,
Tho' the old earth rests, the world is fair.

Opposite page: Springtime at Haweswater.

Now are the mountains winter-white,
Helvellyn shines in the clear moonlight;
The carollers sing, and the Christmas bells
Send sweet messages up the fells;
The old folk meet for their Christmas cheer,
The young folk skate on the frozen mere;
But Spring is coming, the shy buds peep,
The snow-drop moves in her long, long sleep,
The lemon-light shines on the leafless larch,
And the wood grows purple to welcome March.

Fair, how fair, are the changing days
That keep us happy beneath the Raise,
We who, in honour of Oswald the King,
Our 'bearings' still to the Old Church bring,
We who here in the silent time
Act our part and carol our rhyme.
Seasons change, and our hair grows grey,
But merrily goes the Grasmere play,
And two things stay with us all the year –
Love of our valley, and heart of cheer.

H. D. RAWNSLEY

A DUDDON VALLEY FARMSTEAD.

A Well in Langdale

Thou lonely spring of waters undefiled!
Silently slumbering in thy mossy cell,
Yea, moveless as the hillock's verdant side
From which thou had'st thy birth, I bless thy gleam
Of clearest coldness . . .

Thou dost shed
(Though sultry stillness fill the summer air
And parch the yellow hills), all round thy cave,
A smile of beauty lovely as the spring
Breathes with his April showers.

The narrow lane
On either hand ridged with low shelving rocks
That from the roadside gently lead the eye
Up to thy bed . . . a traveller, such as I
Following his fancies o'er these lovely hills
Thankfully here may slake his burning thirst
Once in a season.

Other visitants
It hath not, save perchance the mountain-crow
When ice hath locked the rills, or wandering colt
Leaving its pasture for the shady lane

. . . Flowers are here
Of loveliest colours and of sweetest smell,
Native to these our hills, and ever seen
A fairest family by the happy side
Of their own parent spring . . .

But my soul
Pants for a loftier pleasure
A voice calls on me from the mountain-depths,
And it must be obeyed : yon ledge of rocks,
Like a wild staircase over Hardknots brow,
Is ready for my footsteps and even now,
Wastwater blackens far beneath my feet,
She, the storm-loving lake.

Sweet Fount!–Farewell!

CHRISTOPHER NORTH.

The Heart of May

Now, while the birds thus sing a joyous song,
And while the young lambs bound
As to the tabor's sound,
To me alone there came a thought of grief:
And timely utterance gave that thought relief,
And I again am strong:
The cataracts blow their trumpets from the steep;
No more shall grief of mine the seasons wrong;
I hear the Echoes through the mountains throng,
The Winds come to me from the fields of sleep,
And all the earth is gay;
Land and sea
Give themselves up to jollity,
And with the heart of May
Doth every Beast keep holiday;–
Thou Child of Joy,
Shout round me, let me hear thy shouts, thou happy
Shepherd-boy!

WILLIAM WORDSWORTH
From "Intimations of Immortality."

Opposite: Loweswater Pastoral.

Sunshine and Song

To a Butterfly

Stay near me – do not take thy flight!
A little longer stay in sight!
Much converse do I find in thee,
Historian of my infancy!
Float near me; do not yet depart!
Dead times revive in thee:
Thou bring'st, gay creature as thou art!
A solemn image to my heart,
My father's family!

Oh! pleasant, pleasant were the days,
The time, when, in our childish plays,
My sister Emmeline and I
Together chased the butterfly!
A very hunter did I rush
Upon the prey: – with leaps and springs
I followed on from brake to bush;
But she, God love her, feared to brush
The dust from off its wings.

☆ ☆ ☆

I've watched you now a full half-hour,
Self-poised upon that yellow flower;
And, little Butterfly! indeed
I know not if you sleep or feed.
How motionless! – not frozen seas
More motionless! and then
What joy awaits you, when the breeze
Hath found you out among the trees,
And calls you forth again!

This plot of orchard-ground is ours;
My trees they are, my Sister's flowers;
Here rest your wings when they are weary;
Here lodge as in a sanctuary!
Come often to us, fear no wrong;
Sit near us on the bough!
We'll talk of sunshine and of song,
And summer days, when we were young;
Sweet childish days, that were as long
As twenty days are now.

WILLIAM WORDSWORTH

The Rainbow

My heart leaps up when I behold
  A rainbow in the sky:
So was it when my life began;
So it is now I am a man;
So be it when I shall grow old,
  Or let me die!
The Child is father of the Man;
And I could wish my days to be
Bound each to each by natural piety.

    The Rainbow comes and goes,
    And lovely is the Rose,
    The Moon doth with delight
Look round her when the heavens are bare,
    Waters on a starry night
    Are beautiful and fair;
  The sunshine is a glorious birth;
  But yet I know, Where'er I go:
That there hath past away a glory from the earth.

WILLIAM WORDSWORTH
From "Intimations of Immortality"

☆ ☆ ☆

Oh, there is blessing in this gentle breeze
A vis'tant that while it fans my cheek
Doth seem half-conscious of the joy it brings
From the green fields, and from yon azure sky
What'er its mission, the soft breeze can come
To none more grateful than to me escaped
From the vast city . . .

WILLIAM WORDSWORTH

After the Rain

There was a roaring in the wind all night;
The rain came heavily and fell in floods;
But now the sun is rising calm and bright;
The birds are singing in the distant woods;
Over his own sweet voice the Stock-dove broods;
The Jay makes answer as the Magpie chatters;
And all the air is filled with pleasant noise of waters.

All things that love the sun are out of doors;
The sky rejoices in the morning's birth;
The grass is bright with rain-drops;–on the moors
The Hare is running races in her mirth;
And with her feet she from the plashy earth
Raises a mist; that, glittering in the sun,
Runs with her all the way, whereever she doth run.

WILLIAM WORDSWORTH
From "The Leech-Gatherer"

WINDERMERE

In July

Now has come the month of roses,
Children fill their hands with posies,
All the garden plots are fair,
Honeysuckle scents the air;
Meadow-sweet beside the way
Mingles with the breath of hay,
Rosy loosestrife decks the sedges,
Purple vetch is in the hedges;
Now the butter-wort gives place
To the sundew's jewelled grace;
Now we gather on the fell
Cotton-grass and asphodel;
Bees make music in the limes,
Harebells ring their dainty chimes,
Chimes that only can be heard
When July has hushed the bird.

H. D. RAWNSLEY

August Heather

God, for the gift of the thunder and fire I fear Thee,
– Gift of the thunder and fire that gave us our fells;
But for the gift of this wonder my love comes anear Thee,
Gift of the wonder of these multitudinous bells.

Oh! the sweet scent and the dust of the honey around me –
Oh! the sweet sound of the brindled and golden-thighed bees,
Oh! the content which on Lonscale's round shoulder has found me:
Rest that has found me where body and soul are at ease.

Opposite: Rose Cottage at Outgate.

Blue is the sky, a pavilion with clouds all afeather,
  Green is the plain where the aftermath shimmers and shines,
But purple the million on million of blooms where the heather
  Sweeps rose-ingrain from the blue to the belt of the pines.

Here then on Lonscale I lie, and its garment in splendour
  Grows as the sun sinks, and bees their soft music prolong,
Weariless workers; and I, how can I, any gratitude render,
  Save but by rising from rest with new heart for such labour and song.

H. D. RAWNSLEY

Summer's Ending

The dark green Summer, with its massive hues,
Fades into Autumn's tincture manifold.
A gorgeous garniture of fire and gold
The high slope of the ferny hill indues.
The mists of morn in slumbering layers diffuse
O'er glimmering rock, smooth lake, and spiked array
Of hedge-row thorns a unity of grey.
All things appear their tangible form to lose
In ghostly vastness. But anon the gloom
Melts, as the Sun puts off his muddy veil;
And now the birds their twittering songs resume,
All Summer silent in the leafy dale.
In Spring they piped of love on every tree,
But now they sing the song of memory.

HARTLEY COLERIDGE

VALLEY OF THE ROTHAY.

The Wild Days

Helm Crag

Black is the sky – and every hill –
Up to the sky, is blacker still –
Sky, hill, and dale, one dismal room,
Hung round and overhung with gloom;
Save that above a single height
Is to be seen a lurid light.
Above Helm-crag – a streak half dead,
A burning of portentous red;
And near that lurid light, full well
The ASTROLOGER, sage Sidrophel,
Where at his desk and book he sits,
Puzzling aloft his curious wits;

He whose domain is held in common
With no one but the ANCIENT WOMAN,
Cowering beside her rifted cell,
As if intent on magic spell;–
Dread pair that, spite of wind and weather,
Still sit upon Helm-Crag together.

WILLIAM WORDSWORTH
From "The Waggoner"

Ennerdale

On that tall pike
(It it the loneliest place of all these hills)
There were two springs which bubbled side by side,
As if they had been made that they might be
Companions for each other: the huge crag
Was rent with lightning -- one hath disappeared;
The other, left behind, is flowing still.
For accidents and changes such as these,
We want not store of them;–a waterspout
Will bring down half a mountain; what a feast
For folks that wander up and down . . .
To see an acre's breadth of that wide cliff
One roaring cataract! a sharp May storm
Will come with loads of January snow,
And in one night send twenty score of sheep
To feed the ravens . . .

WILLIAM WORDSWORTH
From "The Brothers"

In Patterdale

The storm is past; the raging wind no more.
Between the mountains rushing, sweeps the vale,
Washing the billows of the troubled lake
High into the air; the snowy fleece lies thick;
From every bough, from every jutting rock
The crystals hang; the torrent's roar has ceased –
As if that Voice that called Creation forth
Had said "Be Still." All nature stands aghast
Suspended by the viewless power of cold.

ELIZABETH SMITH
A poem written in the 18th century

After the Storm

. . . The wind
Was fallen, the rain abated, but the hills
Lay shrouded in impenetrable mist;
. . . homeward the shepherds moved
Through the dull mist, I following – when a step,
A single step, that freed me from the skirts
Of the blind vapour, opened to my view
Glory beyond all glory ever seen
By waking sense or by the dreaming soul!
The appearance, instantaneously disclosed,
Was of a mighty city – boldly say
A wilderness of building, sinking far
And self-withdrawn into a boundless depth,
Far sinking into splendour, without end!

Clouds, mists, streams, watery rocks and emerald turf,
Clouds of all tincture, rocks and sapphire sky,
Confused, commingled, mutually inflamed,
Molten together, and composing thus,
Each lost in each, that marvellous array
Of temple, palace, citadel, and huge
Fantastic pomp of structure without name,
In fleecy folds voluminous enwrapped.

WILLIAM WORDSWORTH

A VIEW FROM GRASMOOR.

In Winter

Skating on Derwentwater

In fairyland we revelled all the day,
Clear-glass of gold lay Derwentwater's flood,
Far Glaramara mailed in silver stood.
And Skiddaw bright for ivory inlay
Shone purple clad with royalest array
  To see our kingly sport. How leapt the blood!
  As on from sunny bay to shadowy wood
We flashed above the mirrors steely grey.

But when the sun o'er Newlands sank to rest
  Enchantment in the valley seemed to grow,
    There, while the snows were flushed on fell
      and moor
    Loud rang the skates upon a lilac floor,
And burning upward thro' the lake's dark breast
  Fire gleamed with unimaginable glow.

H.D. RAWNSLEY.

Skiddaw and Derwentwater

And now am I a Cumbrian mountaineer;
  Their wintry garment of unsullied snow
The mountains have put on, the heavens are clear,
  And yon dark lake spreads silently below;
Who sees them only in their summer hour
Sees but their beauty half, and knows not
      half their power.

ROBERT SOUTHEY.

Grasmere Vale

How calm and beautiful the frosty night
Has stolen unnoticed like the hush of sleep
O'er Grasmere-vale! Beneath the mellowing light
How sinks in softness every rugged steep!
The old church-tower a solemn watch doth keep
O'er the sweet village she adorns so well;
Faintly the freezing stream is heard to weep,
Wild-murmuring far within its icy cell,
And hark! across the lake, clear chimes the
  chapel-bell.

CHRISTOPHER NORTH.

High Ground

Black Comb

This Height a ministering Angel might select:
For from the summit of Black Comb (dread
name
Derived from clouds and storms!) the amplest
range
Of unobstructed prospect may be seen
That British ground commands:–low dusty tracts,
Where Trent is nursed, far southward! Cambrian
Hills
To the south-west, a multitudinous show;
And, in a line of eyesight linked with these,
The hoary peaks of Scotland that gave birth
To Tiviot's stream, to Annan, Tweed, and Clyde:–
Crowding the quarter whence the sun comes forth
Gigantic mountains rough with crags; beneath,
Right at the imperial station's western base,
Main ocean, breaking audibly, and stretched
Far into silent regions blue and pale; –
And visibly engirding Mona's Isle
That, as we left the plain, before our sight
Stood like a lofty mount, uplifting slowly
(Above the convex of the watery globe)
Into clear view the cultured fields that streak
Her habitable shores, but now appears
A dwindled object, and submits to lie
At the spectator's feet.–Yon azure ridge,
Is it a perishable cloud? Or there
Do we behold the line of Erin's coast?
Land sometimes by the roving shepherd swain
(Like the bright confines of another world)
Not doubtfully perceived.–Look homeward now!

In depth, in height, in circuit, how serene
The spectacle, how pure!–Of Nature's works,
In earth, and air, and earth-embracing sea,
A revelation infinite it seems;
Display august of man's inheritance,
Of Britain's calm felicity and power!

WILLIAM WORDSWORTH.

Far off, and half revealed, 'mid shade and light,
Black Comb half smiles, half frowns: his mighty form
Scarce bending into peace, more formed to fight
A thousand years of struggles with a storm
Than bask one hour subdued by sunshine warm
To bright and breezeless rest; yet even his height
Towers not o'er this world's sympathies; he smiles –
While many a human heart to pleasure's wiles
Can bear to bend, and still forget to rise –
As though he, huge and heath-clad on our sight,
Again rejoices in his stormy skies.
Man loses vigour in unstable joys.
Thus tempests find Black Comb invincible,
While we are lost, who should know life so well?

BRANWELL BRONTE.

Opposite: Wetherlam from Little Langdale.

A Faithful Friend

But meeter for thee, gentle lover of nature,
  To lay down thy head like the meek mountain
      lamb,
When, wildered, he drops from some rock high in
      stature,
  And draws his last breath by the side of his dam:
And more stately thy couch by this desert lake lying,
Thy obsequies sung by the gray plover flying,
With but one faithful friend to witness thy dying,
In the arms of Helvellyn and Catchedecam.

WALTER SCOTT.

☆ ☆ ☆

There is a power to bless
In hillside loneliness –
In tarns and dreary places –
A virtue in the brook,
A freshness in the look
Of mountains' joyless faces –
And so, when life is dull
Or when my heart is full
Because my dreams have frowned,
I wander up the rills
To stones and tarns and hills –
I go there to be crowned.

F. W. FABER

Opposite: Evening by Lingmell Beck.

Kirkstone Pass

Most potent when mists veil the sky,
Mists that distort and magnify,
While the coarse rushes, to the sweeping breeze,
Sigh forth their ancient melodies!

List to those shriller notes! *that* march
Perchance was on the blast,
When, through this Height's inverted arch,
Rome's earliest legion passed!
– They saw, adventurously impelled,
And older eyes than theirs beheld,
This block – and yon, whose church-like frame
Gives to this savage Pass its name.
Aspiring Road! that lov'st to hide
Thy daring in a vapoury bourn.

Who comes not hither ne'er shall know
How beautiful the world below;
Nor can he guess how lightly leaps
The brook adown the rocky steeps.

WILLIAM WORDSWORTH

Coniston Old Man

Old man! Old man! your sides are brant,
  And fearfully hard to climb;
My limbs are weak and my breath is scant,
  So I'll rest me here and rhyme.

Yes, my sides are steep, and my dells are deep,
  And my broad bold brow is high,
And you'll ne'er, should you rhyme to the limit of time,
  Find worthier theme than I.

My summit I shroud in the weltering cloud,
  And I laugh at the tempest's din.
I am girdled about with stout rocks without
  And I've countless wealth within.

My silence is broke by the raven's croak,
  And the bark of the mountain fox;
And mine echoes awake to the brown glead's shriek
  As he floats by my hoary rocks.

A. C. GIBSON
A Victorian writer

Helvellyn

I climbed the dark brow of the mighty Helvellyn,
Lakes and mountains beneath me gleamed misty and wide;
All was still – save by fits, when the eagle was yelling,
  And, starting around me, the echoes replied.
On the right, Striding Edge round the Red Tarn was bending,
And Catchedecam its left verge was defending,
One huge nameless rock in front was impending,
  When I marked the sad spot where the wanderer died.

Dark green was that spot, 'mid the brown mountain heather,
  Where the pilgrim of nature lay stretched in decay,
Like the corpse of an outcast, abandoned to weather,
  Till the mountain winds wasted the tenantless clay:
Not yet quite deserted, though lonely extended,
For faithful in death, his mute favourite attended,
The much loved remains of his master defended,
  And chased the hill-fox and the raven away.

How long did'st thou think that his silence was slumber –
  When the wind waved his garments how oft didst thou start –
How many long days and long nights didst thou number,
  Ere he faded before thee, the friend of thy heart?–
And, ah! was it meet that no requiem read o'er him;
No mother to weep, and no friend to deplore him;
And thou, little guardian, alone stretched before him,
  Unhonoured the pilgrim from life should depart?

When a prince to the fate of a peasant has yielded,
  The tapestry waves dark round the dim-lighted hall;
With escutcheons of silver the coffin is shielded,
  And the pages stand mute by the canopied pall;
  Through the courts, at deep midnight, the torches are gleaming,

Opposite: Striding Edge, Helvellyn.

In the proudly arched chapel the banners are beaming,
Far adown the long aisle sacred music is streaming,
  Lamenting a chief of the people should fall.

WALTER SCOTT

Jutting Rocks

A mount, not wearisome and bare and steep,
  But a green mountain variously up-piled,
Where o'er the jutting rocks soft mosses creep,
Or coloured lichens with slow oozing weep;
  Where cypress and the darker yew start wild;
And 'mid the summer torrent's gentle dash
Dance brightened the red clusters of the ash;
  Beneath whose boughs, by those still sounds beguiled,
Calm Pensiveness might muse herself to sleep.

SAMUEL TAYLOR COLERIDGE

Opposite: High Spy, from Derwent's banks.

Near Grasmere

No habitation can be seen; but they
Who journey thither find themselves alone
With a few sheep, with rocks and stones, and kites
That overhead are sailing in the sky.
It is in truth an utter solitude.

WILLIAM WORDSWORTH
Writing of Green-head Ghyll

Helm Crag

Go up among the mountains, when the storm
Of midnight howls, but go in that wild mood,
When the soul loves tumultuous solitude,
And through the haunted air, each giant form
Of swinging pine, black rock, or ghostly cloud,
That veils some fearful cataract tumbling loud,
Seems to thy breathless heart with life imbued.
'Mid those gaunt, shapeless things thou art alone!
The mind exists, trembles through the ear,
The memory of the human world is gone
And time and space seem living only *here*.

CHRISTOPHER NORTH

Blue Hills

There is a thrill of strange delight
   That passes quivering o'er me,
When blue hills rise upon the sight
   Like summer clouds before me.

JOHN RUSKIN
Written when he was 14 years of age

Armboth Fells

And now, in front behold outspread
Those upper regions we must tread;
Mild hollows, and clear heathy swells
The cheery silence of the fells.

MATTHEW ARNOLD
From "Resignation"

Castlerigg

. . . like a dismal cirque
Of Druid stones, upon a forlorn moor,
When the chill rain begins at shut of eve,
In dull November, and their chancel vault,
The Heaven itself, is blinded throughout night.

JOHN KEATS
From "Hyperion"

Opposite: On Dalehead above Honister.

Blencathra

On mountain, moss, and moor.
Above his solitary track
Rose huge Blencathra's ridgy back,
Amid whose yawning gulfs the sun
Cast umber'd radiance red and dun,
Though never sunbeam could discern
The surface of that stable tarn
In whose dark mirror you may spy
The stars, while noontide lights the sky.

WALTER SCOTT
The "Sable Tarn" is Scales Tarn

Small and Silent

A green and silent spot, amid the hills,
A small and silent dell! O'er stiller place
No singing sky-lark ever poised himself.
The hills are heathy, save that swelling slope,
Which hath a gay and gorgeous covering on,
All golden with the never-bloomless furze,
Which now blooms most profusely: but the dell,
Bathed by the mist, is fresh and delicate
As vernal cornfield, or the unripe flax,
When, through its half-transparent stalks, at eve,
The level sunshine glimmers with green light.
O! 'tis quiet spirit-healing nook!
Which all, methinks, would love.

SAMUEL T. COLERIDGE

Not with the mean and
vulgar works of man,
But with high objects,
with enduring things.
WILLIAM WORDSWORTH

She welcomed what was
given, and
craved no more.
Whatever scene was present
to her eyes,
That was the best.
WILLIAM WORDSWORTH

How frowned the dark rocks
which, bare, savage
and wild,
In heaps upon heaps were
tremendously piled
JOHN RUSKIN

There sometimes doth a leaping fish
Send through the tarn a lonely cheer.
WILLIAM WORDSWORTH

Thither the rainbow
comes — the cloud —
And mists that spread
the flying shroud.

WILLIAM WORDSWORTH

Thy roofs, O Keswick,
brighter rise,
The lake, and lofty
hills between
Where giant Skiddaw
shuts the scene.

JOHN DALTON

No sound is uttered, —
but a deep
And solemn harmony
pervades
The hollow vale from
steep to steep.

WILLIAM WORDSWORTH

The crags repeat the
raven's croak,
In symphony austere.

WILLIAM WORDSWORTH

. . . lustily
I dipped my oars into the
silent lake,
And, as I rose upon the stroke,
my boat
Went heaving through the water
like a swan.

WILLIAM WORDSWORTH

. . . in seeming silence
makes
A soft eye — music of
slow-waving boughs
WILLIAM WORDSWORTH

Sparkling Water

Windermere in November

Do mark, reflected by the glorious sun,
Those oozing streams, o'er rocky smoothness run,
The heath's dun shade, the lately-wither'd fern,
The woods, all fancy, and the mountains stern.
Now inward turn, far as the Lake extends,
Whose lessen'd breadth with quicker pace descends,

To where . . . a bird's eye view commands
Those rugged mountains, of stupendous form;
Whose savage foreheads frown amidst a storm;
Whence, to the South, with pensiveness survey
The verdant surface of the boundless sea.
Now view the Lake, whose placid bosom shows
The smallest twig that on her margin grows
Th' inverted hills and mountains far and near,
From their own base all crystalliz'd appear.

Yet, when I think of the retreating year,
The heart could almost give the eye a tear
To see the islands, and the trees below,
Whose beauties soon must be replaced by snow
From lofty Skiddaw, and Helvellyn proud,
The hills, like waves, irregularly crowd;
From savage Langdale, whence no tree is seen
To cheer the longing eye with healthful green.

JOSEPH BUDWORTH.
Part of a poem written in 1798.

Loughrigg Tarn

How soft these fields of pastoral beauty melt
In the clear water! neither sand nor stone
Bars herb or wild-flower from the dewy sound,
Like Spring's own voice now rippling round the
Tarn.
Guards thee;–and wooded knolls fantastical
Seclude thy image from the gentler dale,
That by the Brathay's often-varied voice
Cheered as it winds along, in beauty fades
'Mid the green banks of joyful Windermere!
The hours
Passed tranquilly with Nature fade not away
For ever like the clouds, but in the soul
Possess a secret silent dwelling-place,
Where, with a smiling visage, memory sits.
. . . Sweet Lake
Oft hast thou borne into my grateful heart
Thy lovely presence, with a thousand dreams
Dancing and brightening o'er thy sunny wave,
Though many a dreary mile of mist and snow
Between us interposed.

CHRISTOPHER NORTH.

Prospect of Windermere

A dreary moor
Was crossed; a bare ridge clomb, upon whose
    top
Standing alone, as from a rampart's edge,
I overlooked the bed of Windermere,
  Like a vast river, stretching in the sun.
  With exultation, at my feet I saw
Lake, islands, promontories, gleaming bays,
A universe of Nature's fairest forms
Proudly revealed with instantaneous burst,
Magnificent, and beautiful and gay.

WILLIAM WORDSWORTH.
From "The Prelude."

Near Blea Tarn

Urn-like it was in shape, deep as an urn;
With rocks encompassed, save that to the south
Was one small opening, where a heath-clad ridge
Supplied a boundary less abrupt and close;
A quiet treeless nook, with two green fields,
A liquid pool that glittered in the sun,
And one bare dwelling. . . .
                                        Full many a spot
Of hidden beauty have I chanced to espy
Among the mountains; never one like this
So lonesome, and so perfectly secure;
Not melancholy–no, for it is green
And bright and fertile . . .
–In rugged arms how softly does it lie.

WILLIAM WORDSWORTH.
From "The Excursion."

Wastwater

Is this the lake, the cradle of the storms,
Where silence never tames the mountain-roar,
Where poets fear their self-created forms,
Or, sunk in trance severe, their God adore?
Is this the lake for ever dark and loud,
With wave and tempest, cataract and cloud?
Wondrous, O Nature, is thy sovereign power,
That gives to horror hours of peaceful mirth;
For here might beauty build her summer bower!
Lo! where yon rainbow spans the smiling earth,
And clothed in glory, through a silent shower
The mighty Sun comes forth, a god-like birth;
While, 'neath his loving eye the gentle Lake
Lies like a sleeping child too blest to wake!

CHRISTOPHER NORTH

Grasmere

O Vale and lake, within your mountain-urn
Smiling so tranquilly, and set so deep!
Oft doth your dreamy loveliness return,
Colouring the tender shadows of my sleep
With light Elysian; for the hues that steep
Your shores in melting lustre, seem to float
On golden clouds from spirit-lands remote,
Isles of the blest; and in our memory keep
Their place with holiest harmonies. Fair scene,
Most loved by evening and her dewy star!
Oh! ne'er may man, with touch unhallowed, jar
The perfect music of thy charm serene!
Still, still unchanged, may *one* sweet region wear
Smiles that subdue the soul to love, and tears, and
prayer.

FELICIA DOROTHEA HEMANS.

Opposite: Wastwater.

A FELL BECK.

Lodore

From its sources which well
    In the Tarn on the fell;
    From its fountains
    In the mountains,
    Its rills and its gills;
Through moss and through brake,
    It runs and it creeps
    For awhile till it sleeps
    In its own little Lake.

And thence at departing,
Awakening and starting,
It runs through the reeds
      And away it proceeds,
Through meadow and glade,
      In sun and in shade,
And through the wood-shelter,
      Among crags in its flurry,
         Helter-skelter,
         Hurry-scurry.
Here it comes sparkling,
And there it lies darkling;
Now smoaking and frothing
      Its tumult and wrath in,
      Till in this rapid race
      On which it is bent,
      It reaches the place
      Of its steep descent.
      The Cataract strong
      Then plunges along,
      Striking and raging
      As if a war waging
Its caverns and rocks among:
      Rising and leaping
      Sinking and creeping,
      Swelling and sweeping,
Showering and springing,
      Flying and flinging,
      Writhing and ringing,
      Eddying and whisking,
      Spouting and frisking,
      Turning and twisting,
      Around and around
      With endless rebound!
      Smiting and fighting,
      A sight to delight in;
      Confounding, astounding,

Dizzying and deafening the ear with its sound.
Collecting, projecting,
Receding and speeding,
And shocking and rocking,
And darting and parting,
And threading and spreading,
And whizzing and hissing,
And dripping and skipping,
And hitting and splitting,
And shining and twining,
And rattling and battling,
And shaking and quaking,
And pouring and roaring,
And waving and raving,
And tossing and crossing,
And flowing and going,
And running and stunning,
And foaming and roaming,
And dinning and spinning,
And dropping and hopping,
And working and jerking,
And guggling and struggling,
And heaving and cleaving,
And moaning and groaning;
And glittering and frittering,
And gathering and feathering,
And whitening and brightening,
And quivering and shivering,
And hurrying and scurrying,
And thundering and floundering,
Dividing and gliding and sliding,
And falling and brawling and sprawling,
And diving and riving and striving,
And sprinkling and twinkling and wrinkling,
And sounding and bounding and rounding,
And bubbling and troubling and doubling,

And grumbling and rumbling and tumbling,
And clattering and battering and shattering;
Retreating and beating and meeting and sheeting,
Delaying and straying and playing and spraying,
Advancing and prancing and glancing and dancing,
Recoiling, turmoiling and toiling and boiling,
And gleaming and streaming and steaming and beaming,
And rushing and flushing and brushing and gushing,
And flapping and rapping and clapping and slapping,
And curling and whirling and purling and twirling,
And thumping and plumping and bumping and jumping,
And dashing and flashing and splashing and clashing;
And so never ending, but always descending,
Sounds and motions for ever and ever are blending,
All at once and all o'er with a mighty uproar,
And this way the water comes down at Lodore.

ROBERT SOUTHEY
From "Rhymes for the Nursery", 1820

Aira Force

Not a breath of air
Ruffles the bosom of this leafy glen.
From the brook's margin, wide around, the trees
Are steadfast as the rocks; the brook itself,
Old as the hills that feed it from afar,
Doth rather deepen than disturb the calm
Where all things else are still and motionless.
And yet, even now, a little breeze, perchance
Escaped from boisterous winds that rage without

Has entered by the sturdy oaks unfelt,
But to its gentle touch how sensitive
Is the light ash! that, pendent from the brow
Of yon dim cave, in seeming silence makes
A soft eye-music of slow-waving boughs,
Powerful almost as vocal harmony
To stay the wanderer's steps and soothe his thoughts.

WILLIAM WORDSWORTH.

Grasmere

The valley stretched
In length before us; and, not distant far,
Upon a rising ground, a grey church-tower,
Whose battlements were screened by tufted trees.
And towards a crystal Mere, that lay beyond
Among steep hills and woods embosomed, flowed
A copious stream with boldly-winding course;
Here traceable, there hidden – there again
To sight restored, and glittering in the sun.

WILLIAM WORDSWORTH

Opposite: Aira Force.

There was a Boy

There was a Boy: ye knew him well, ye cliffs
And islands of Winander!–many a time
At evening, when the earliest stars began
To move along the edges of the hills,
Rising or setting, would he stand alone
Beneath the trees or by the glimmering lake,
And there, with fingers interwoven, both hands
Pressed closely palm to palm, and to his mouth
Uplifted, he, as through an instrument,
Blew mimic hootings to the silent owls,
That they might answer him; and they would shout
Across the watery vale, and shout again,
Responsive to his call, with quivering peals,
And long halloos and screams, and echoes loud,
Redoubled and redoubled, concourse wild
Of jocund din; and, when a lengthened pause
Of silence came and baffled his best skill,
Then sometimes, in that silence while he hung
Listening, a gentle shock of mild surprise
Has carried far into his heart the voice
Of mountain torrents; or the visible scene
Would enter unawares into his mind,
With all its solemn imagery, its rocks,
Its woods, and that uncertain heaven, received
Into the bosom of the steady lake.

WILLIAM WORDSWORTH.
From "The Prelude."

Opposite: Windermere at Waterhead.

The Mountain Rill

Shall I sing of little rills,
That trickle down the yellow hills,
To drive the Fairies' water-mills?–
Rills, upon whose pebbly brink,
Mountain birds may hop and drink–
Perching with a neck awry–
Darting upwards to the sky
The artless cunning of their eye–
Then away, away, away–
Up to the clouds that look so grey,
Away, away, in the clear blue heaven,
Far o'er the thin mist that beneath is driven–
Now they sink, and now they soar,
Now poised upon the plumy oar,
Do they seek–at brightest noon,
For the light-inveiled moon?

Climbing upwards would they know
Where the stars at morning go?
If I err not-no-no-no-
Soar they high, or skim they low,
Every bird has still
His heart beside the mountain rill.

HARTLEY COLERIDGE.

Red Tarn, Helvellyn

It was a cove, a huge recess,
That keeps, till June, December's snow;
A lofty precipice in front,
A silent tarn below!
Far in the bosom of Helvellyn,
Remote from public road or dwelling,
Pathway, or cultivated land;
From trace of human foot or hand.

There sometimes doth a leaping fish
Send through the tarn a lonely cheer;
The crags repeat the raven's croak,
In symphony austere;
Thither the rainbow comes–the cloud–
And mists that spread the flying shroud;
And sunbeams; and the sounding blast,
That, if it could, would hurry past;
But that enormous barrier holds it fast.

WILLIAM WORDSWORTH.
From "Fidelity."

Coniston Water

With its deep-bosomed billows in front lay the lake,
Whose waters divided by mountain and cape,
All open and bare they, full lonely did lie,
Exposing their breast to the shadowy sky:
Retiring in distance they mistily lay;
And fainter each inlet, and softer each bay;
Till, appearing no more, by the wild tempest tost,
'Mid mountains and clouds in the distance were lost.

JOHN RUSKIN.

To a child

Small service is true service while it
lasts:
Of humblest Friends, bright Creature!
scorn not one:
The Daisy, by the shadow that it casts,
Protects the lingering dew-drop from the
Sun.

WILLIAM WORDSWORTH.
A composition written in an album, 1834.

Wild Creatures

A Raven's Cry

. . . and often, at the hour
When issue forth the first pale stars, is heard
Within the circuit of this fabric huge,
One voice – the solitary raven, flying
Athwart the concave of the dark blue dome,
Unseen, perchance above all power of sight –
An iron knell! with echoes from afar
Faint – and still fainter – as the cry, with which
The wanderer accompanies her flight
Through the calm region, fades upon the ear,
Diminishing by distance till it seemed
To expire; yet from the abyss is caught again,
And yet again recovered!

WILLIAM WORDSWORTH.
He was fascinated by the raven.

An Evening Walk

Sweet are the sounds that mingle from afar,
Heard by calm lakes, as peeps the folding star,
Where the duck dabbles 'mid the rustling sedge,
And feeding pike starts from the water's edge,
Or the swan stirs the reeds, his neck and bill
Wetting, that drip upon the water still;
And heron, as resounds the trodden shore,
Shoots upward, darting his long neck before.

WILLIAM WORDSWORTH.

The Redbreast

When winter winds blow strang and keen,
  An' neets are lang an' cauld,
An' flocks o' burds, we' famine team't,
  Come flutteren into t'fauld;
I hev a casement, just ya pane,
  'At Robin kens reet weel,
An' pops in meeny a time i 't'day,
  A crumb or two to steal.

At furst he's shy an' easy flay't,
  Bit seunn he bolder gits,
An' picks aboot quite unconsarn't,
  Or here an' theer he flits.
An' when he gits his belly full,
  An' stir't o' playin' pranks,
He'll sit quite still, on t'auld chair back,
  An' sing his simple thanks.

Bit when breet spring comes back ageann,
  An' fields ur growen green,
He bids good day, an' flees away,
  An' than na mair he's seen;
Till winter comes ageann wi' frost,
An' driften snow, an' rain,
An' than he venters back ageann,
  To leuk for t'oppen pane.

Noo, burds an' fwok ur mickle t'seamm,
  If they be i' hard need;
An' yan hes owt to give, they'll come,
  An' be girt frinds indeed.
Bit when theer nowt they want to hev,
  It's nut sa lang they'll stay,
Bit just as Robin does i' t' spring,
  They'll seun aw flee away.

JOHN RICHARDSON.

Glow-worms

Among all lovely things my Love had been;
Had noted well the stars, all flowers that grew
About her home; but she had never seen
A Glow-worm, never one, and this I knew.

While riding near her home one stormy night
A single Glow-worm did I chance to espy;
I gave a fervent welcome to the sight,
And from my Horse I leapt; great joy had I.

Upon a leaf the Glow-worm did I lay,
To bear it with me through the stormy night:
And, as before, it shone without dismay;
Albeit putting forth a fainter light.

When to the Dwelling of my Love I came,
I went into the Orchard quietly;
And left the Glow-worm, blessing it by name,
Laid safely by itself, beneath a Tree.

The whole next day I hoped, and hoped with fear;
At night the Glow-worm shone beneath the Tree:
I led my Lucy to the spot, 'Look here!'
Oh! joy it was for her, and joy for me!

WILLIAM WORDSWORTH

The Country Folk

An Aged Man

I rose and turned towards a group of trees
Which midway in that level stood alone,
And thither came at length beneath a shade
Of clustering elms that sprang from the same root
I found a ruined Cottage – four clay walls
That stared upon each other. 'Twas a spot
The wandering Gypsey in a stormy night
Would pass it with his moveables to house
On the open plain beneath the imperfect arch
Of a cold lime-kiln. As I looked around

Beside the door I saw an aged Man
Stretched on a bench whose edge with short bright moss
Was green, and studded o'er with fungus flowers.
An iron-pointed staff lay at his side.
Him had I seen the day before, alone
And in the middle of the public way
Standing to rest himself. His eyes were turned
Towards the setting sun, while, with that staff
Behind him fixed, he propped a long white pack
Which crossed his shoulders; wares for maids who live
In lonely villages or straggling huts.
I knew him – he was born of lowly race
On Cumbrian hills, and I have seen the tear
Stand in his luminous eye when he described
The house in which his early youth was passed
And found I was no stranger to the spot.
I loved to hear him talk of former days
And tell how when a child, ere yet of age
To be a shepherd, he had learned to read
His bible in a school that stood alone,
Sole building on a mountain's dreary edge,
Far from the sight of city spire, or sound
Of Minster clock. From that bleak tenement
He many an evening to his distant home
In solitude returning saw the hills
Grow larger in the darkness, all alone
Beheld the stars come out above his head,
And travelled through the wood, no comrade near,
To whom he might confess the things he saw.
So the foundations of his mind were laid
In such communion, not from terror free . . .

WILLIAM WORDSWORTH.
From "The Ruined Cottage."

Bells of Borrowdale

Each matin Bell, the Baron saith,
Knells us back to a world of death,
These words Sir Leoline first said,
When he rose and found his lady dead:
These words Sir Leoline will say
Many a morn to his dying day!

And hence the custom and law began
That still at dawn the sacristan,
Who duly pulls the heavy bell
Five and forty beads must tell
Between each stroke – a warning knell,
Which not a soul can choose but hear
From Bratha Head to Wyndermere.

Saith Bracy the bard. So let it knell!
And let the drowsy sacristan
Still count as slowly as he can!
There is no lack of such, I ween,
As well fill up the space between.
In Langdale Pike and Witch's Lair,
And Dungeon-ghyll so foully rent,
With ropes of rock and bells of air
Three sinful sextons' ghosts are pent,
Who all give back, one after t'other,
The death-note to their living brother;
And oft too, by the knell offended,
Just as their one! two! three! is ended,
The devil mocks the doleful tale
With a merry peal from Borodale.

SAMUEL TAYLOR COLERIDGE.
From "Christabel."

Clipping Time

Underneath the sycamore
Shepherds count their fleecy store,
Neighbours come from far and near,
Neighbour-like the flock to shear,
Here the urchin fresh from school
Helps to load the clipping stool,
Holds the tie for legs that kick,
Hands the tarry "smitting" stick.
Very grave the grey-beards seem
Tho' the bright shears click and gleam,
And the girls with laughter soft
Toss the fleeces to the loft,
While the little children run
To and fro in ceaseless fun.

Bark of dogs is in our ears,
And beneath the magic shears
Lo! the creature dumb from fright
Turns from tawny into white.
Then, at last set free, the sheep
From the clipping stool will leap,
While the lambs with plaintive cries
Greet their mother's new surprise,
And the dogs as wise as men
Push their charge from pen to pen.

H. D. RAWNSLEY.
From "July at the Lakes."

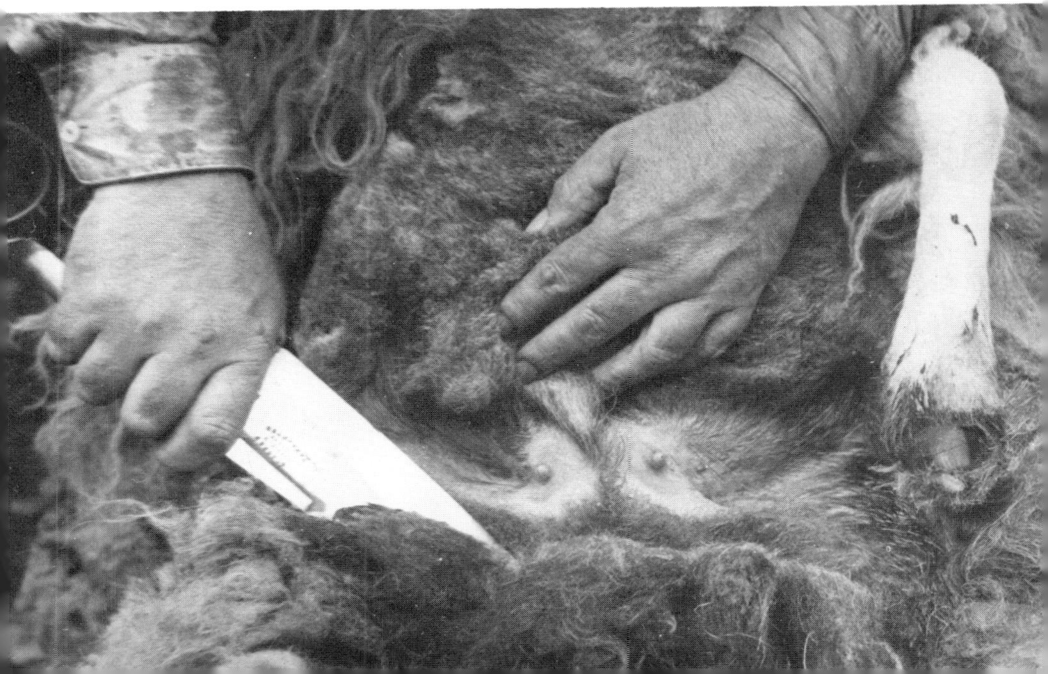

John Peel

Did you ken John Peel with his coat so gray?
Did ye ken John Peel at the break o' the day?
Did ye ken John Peel go far far away?
  With his hounds and his horns in a morning.

Chorus:
For the sound of the horn called me from my bed,
And the cry of the hounds me oft has led,
John Peel's view hallo would waken the dead,
  Or a fox from his lair in the morning.

Did ye ken John Peel both oft and far,
O'er rasper fence, and the gate and the bar,
From Low Denton Holme up to Scratchmere Scar,
  When you strove for the brush in the morning?

Oh, yes, I have seen and done far more,
And many a time, as I did tell o'er,
How we ran into foxes in galore,
  Ere the hoar left the hills in a morning?

Did ye ken that hound, whose tongue was death?
Did ye ken her sons of peerless faith?
Did ye ken that a fox, with his last breath,
  Curs'd them as he died in a morning?

And I kenn'd John Peel, and auld Ruby, too,
Ranter and Royal, and Bellman as true.
From the drag to the chase, from chase to the view,
From the view to the death in a morning.

Here's to John Peel, with my heart and my soul,
Come fill, O fill to him another bowl,
And we'll follow John Peel thro' fair and foul,
While we're waked by his horn in the morning.

JOHN WOODCOCK GRAVES.
An Early Version of the Famous Song.

Buttermere Round

From Keswick Town to Borrowdale
    Beneath the loud Lodore
I take my team through Derwent Vale,
    My staunch and dauntless four;
By Falcon Crag and Castle Hill
    Their lead-bars lift and swing,
And stepping with a right good will
    They make the lake-road ring.

By farm and church and lone hotel
    They thread the narrowing way
Till, closing inward, peak and fell
    Rise round us gaunt and grey.
And up the arduous path they go
    With shoulders collar-strained
Till, the last larchwood left below,
    The crown at last is gained.

Down the high crag of Honister
    The tinkling slate stone falls
From where unseen the quarrier
    Toils on its steep grey walls;
And circling round its rampart crest
    The great hawks dive and climb
In that unending mountain quest
    That takes no heed of time.

The shadows on the peaks are blue,
    The rock ravines are black;
We sink the hill with chain and "shoe"
    And collars riding slack
Till safely through the outcrop slate
    The team with jingling gear
Takes up the road by bank and gate
    That leads to Buttermere.

Opposite: Stonethwaite Beck.

Watered and rested, groomed and fed,
    Once more with straining bars
They face the winding steeps ahead
    As though to climb the stars;
Once more the high tops left and right,
    Once more the mists of blue;
Once more the pause upon the height,
    Once more the chain and shoe.

And so we pass the hills of charm
    That slope on either hand
And, swinging down by fold and farm,
    Come back to planted land;
And through the shades of Portinscale,
    By Greta's guiding stream,
The children on the pathway hail
    My tired head-tossing team.

But they've a price to hold and keep
    And they've a trust to bear;
The road was long, the passes steep,
    But each has pulled his share;
And now, heads high, with quickened pace
    Arched necks and lifted knees
They thunder through the market-place
    As proudly as you please.

From Keswick Town to Windermere
    And round the Thirlmere ring
From Bassenthwaite to Bowness Pier
    The Carburettor's King;
But we can climb where engines fail
    And, conquerors of the crest,
We rule the road from Borrowdale
    To where the brown hawks nest.

W. H. OGILVY.

Opposite: Buttermere.

Cumbrian Pride

Canny Cummerlan'

Yer Buik-larn'd wise gentry, that's seen monie
  counties,
May preach and palaver, and brag as they will
O' mountains, lakes, valleys, woods, watters, and
  meadows,
  But canny auld Cummerlan caps them aw still:
It's true, we've nae palaces sheynin amang us,
  Nor marble tall towers to catch the weak eye;
But we've monie feyne cassels, where fit our brave
  fadders,
  When Cummerland cud onie county defy.

Whea that hes climb'd Skiddaw, has seen sec a
  prospec,
  Where fells frown owre fells, and in majesty vie?
Whea that hes seen Keswick, can count hawf its
  beauties,
  May e'en try to count hawf the stars i' the sky:
Theer's Ullswater, Bassenthwaite, Wastwater,
  Derwent,
  That thousands on thousands ha'e travell'd to
  view;
The langer they gaze, still the mair they may wonder,
  And ay, as they wonder, may fin summet new.

ROBERT ANDERSON.
"The Cumbrian Bard."
A composition of about 1820.

Opposite: Ullswater, with Place Fell.

A Westmorland Song

Rust-red are the mountains
  And white fall the fountains
  When over Helvellyn fly wintry gales;
But green when the comer,
Who brings us the summer,
    The cuckoo calls clear o'er the Westmorland
      dales.

When bracken was springing
The live air was ringing,
    The lambs with loud chorus filled valleys
      below;
Now bracken is umber,
How deep is the slumber
    Of mountains that wait for the silence of snow.

But oh! for the weather
That brought us the heather,
    When high Pike o' Stickle and Easdale were
      bright;
And oh! the long gloamings
Of May, for the roamings
    O'er hills that were never quite darkened with
        night.

Ye Westmorland mountains,
Ye Westmorland fountains,
    The clouds are your children, the streams are
        your birth;
When tear-drops fall quickly,
And clouds gather thickly,
    Your calm and your hope bring new comfort
        to Earth.

H. D. RAWNSLEY.

The Fuller Life

Wythburn Chapel

Here, traveller, pause and think, and duly think
   What happy, holy thoughts may heavenward
      rise,
Whilst thou and thy good steed together drink
   Beneath this little portion of the skies.

See! on one side, a humble house of prayer,
   Where Silence dwells, a maid immaculate,
Save when the Sabbath and the priest are there,
   And some few hungry souls for manna wait.

Humble it is and meek and very low,
  And speaks its purpose by a single bell;
But God Himself, and He alone, can know
  If spiry temples please Him half so well.

Then see the World, the world in its best guise,
  Inviting thee its bounties to partake;
Dear is the Sign's old time-discolour'd dyes
  To weary trudger by the long black lake.

And pity 'tis that other studded door
  That looks so rusty right across the way,
Stands not always as was the use of yore,
  That whoso passes may step in and pray.

HARTLEY COLERIDGE.

Intimations of Immortality

Our birth is but a sleep and a forgetting:
      The Soul that rises with us, our life's Star,
    Hath had elsewhere its setting,
    And cometh from afar:
    Not in entire forgetfulness,
    And not in utter nakedness,
But trailing clouds of glory do we come
    From God, who is our home:
Heaven lies about us in our infancy!
Shades of the prison-house begin to close
    Upon the growing Boy,
But He beholds the light, and whence it flows,
    He sees it in his joy;

The Youth, who daily farther from the east
Must travel, still is Nature's Priest,
And by the vision splendid
Is on his way attended;
At length the Man perceives it die away,
And fade into the light of common day.

Oh joy! that in our embers
Is something that doth live,
That Nature yet remembers
What was so fugitive!
. . . I raise
The song of thanks and praise;
. . . For those first affections
Those shadowy recollections,
Which, be they what they may,
Are yet the fountain-light of all our day,
Are yet a master-light of all our seeing;
Uphold us, cherish, and have power to make
Our noisy years seem moments in the being
Of the eternal Silence–

WILLIAM WORDSWORTH.

There was a time when meadow, grove and stream,
The earth and every common sight,
To me did seem
Apparelled in celestial light,
The glory and the freshness of a dream,
It is not now as it hath been of yore;–
Turn wheresoe'er I may,
By night or day,
The things which I have seen I now can see no more.

WILLIAM WORDSWORTH.

. . . Backward, Duddon, as I cast my eyes,
I see what was, and is, and will abide;
The Form remains, the Function never dies;
While we, the brave, the mighty and the wise,
We Men, who in our morn of youth defied
The elements, must vanish;– be it so!

Enough, if something from our hands have power
To live, and act, and serve the future hour;
And if, as towards the silent tomb we go,
Through love, through hope, and faith's transcendent
dower,
We feel that we are greater than we know.

WILLIAM WORDSWORTH.
From "The River Duddon."

The Dear Hills

Dear native regions, I foretell,
From what I feel at this farewell,
That, wheresoe'er my steps may tend,
And whensoe'er my course shall end,
If in that hour a single tie
Survive of local sympathy,
My soul will cast the backward view,
The longing look alone on you.

Thus, while the Sun sinks down to rest
Far in the regions of the west,
Though to the vale no parting beam
Be given, not one memorial gleam,
A lingering light he fondly throws
On the dear hills where first he rose.

WILLIAM WORDSWORTH.
At the age of 16 years.

Index to Poems